THE
BLUEPRINT

CREDIT

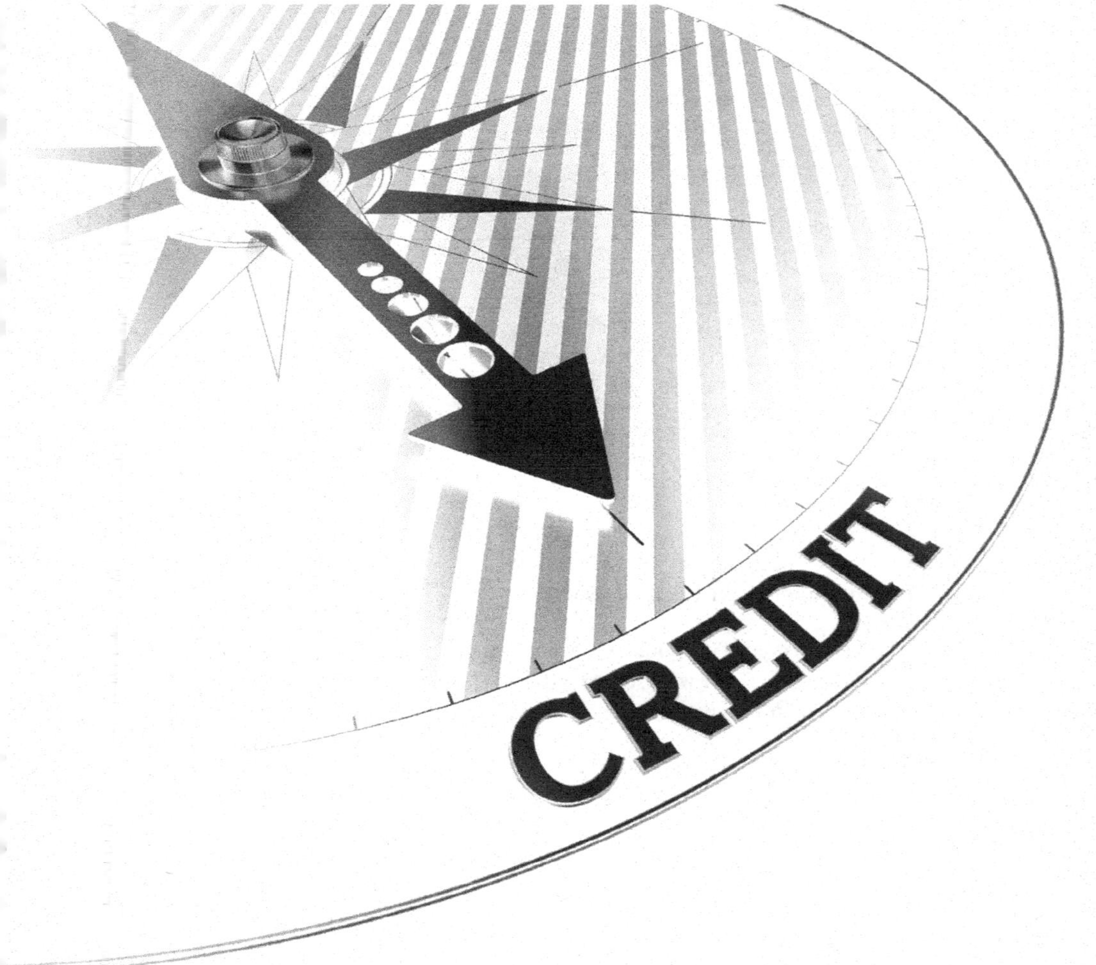

CARRESSA WALKER

ISBN: 978-1-66781-210-6

Table of Contents

Definition Of a Credit

A credit is an advance of money. You must ensure your repayment and capacity and don't forget to consider the duration of your commitment. There are different types of credit; the bank will work with you to find the most suitable formula for your situation.

To Incur an Expense When You Don't Have Enough Money

Either you save and delay spending until you have accumulated enough cash or borrow the sum necessary to carry out the expenditure immediately. You will repay the credit as you go—the amount loaned, plus interest.

The credit allows you to incur an expense now that you will repay later (often gradually) and with the payment of interest. It saves you from waiting until you have saved the necessary amount.

We Can Distinguish the Credit for Consumption and Housing Loans By

- **Duration-** Generally, consumer loans tend to be short-term loans. Mortgage loans are relatively long-term loans (ten to fifteen years or even more), although we also find in this category bridging loans that can last less than two years.

The Object of Credit

A consumer credit used to finance everyday life and equipment expenses, or large expenses like cars and boats. A mortgage makes it possible to finance the acquisition of land or housing or even renovation or development work.

The Choice of a Suitable Credit

There are different types of credit to the consumer and mortgage. You will generally have to carry out with your bank advisor several simulations before finding the right formula or sometimes the correct procedures. It is not uncommon, especially when it comes to mortgage loans, that the solution involves a combination of several credits.

Your advisor will help you find the best solution based on:

- **The purchase you want to make**
- **The amount you need**
- **Your situation**

Types Or Names of Credit

1. Credit with Depreciation

The most common type of borrowing is depreciable credit. It can be used to buy a consumer good or a service—in which case it is referred to as a consumer credit— or it can be used to purchase real estate. It is a mortgage in this case. A depreciable credit can be granted at both fixed and variable interest rates. Its distinguishing feature is that each maturity repays both interest and a portion of the borrowed capital (this is the amortization of the money). It is a generic term, as opposed to credit in fine (with term repayment).

2. The Variable-Rate Loan

The interest rate on an adjustable-rate credit (also known as variable rate) is indexed and can thus move up or down. This automatic rate change may affect either the repayment period or the monthly payment (or both). A limited rate is the one in which the rate variation is little in comparison to the initial rate.

3. Adaptable Credit

The term "flexible" refers to the subscriber's ability to increase or decrease his monthly payments, delay one or more, or make a partial early repayment. Home loans, whether at fixed rate or adjustable rate, are typically flexible loans.

4. Credit with a Fixed-Interest Repayment Schedule

Individuals do not commonly use this credit formula. It's more suited to professionals or specific financial arrangements. Each maturity of constant capital repayment credit is used to repay the same amount of capital. In practice, this means that the monthly payment will decrease over time. The total amount due (reimbursed capital + interest) gradually decreases over time as interest is calculated on the outstanding money.

Compared to a fixed-term loan of the same amount and the same duration, this loan has a lower overall cost.

The following form allows you to calculate your monthly payments. A schedule is automatically generated. Use the following website to access the online calculation form: https://www.bankrate.calculators/home-equity/loan-repayment-calculator.aspx.aspx

5. Fixed-Rate Credit with Maturities That Increase Over Time

Not to be confused with a rate that can be changed. The maturity of this credit is increased by a certain percentage each year to allow for amortization. The monthly payment may rise by one percent per year, for example.

It allows for smaller monthly payments at the start of repayments when compared to a constant maturity loan. Credit with progressive maturity will be more expensive than credit with constant maturity at the same interest rate (or TEG).

6. Credit in Fine

Unlike a repayable loan, the monthly loan payments in fine only reimburse the interest and not the borrowed capital (and, if applicable, the insurance). At the final installment, the money will be refunded in full. This type of credit is commonly used in the context of rental investments.

7. The Bridging Credits

The bridging credit makes it possible to finance a new acquisition when the old housing has not yet been sold. It is a loan in a fine that does not speak its name and makes the connection in the financing until the recovery of the money of the sale. By nature, the duration of the bridging loan is short.

8. Pawnbroker

The pawnshop is a credit granted in return for a property left as collateral. This type is also known as a secured loan.

Role Of Credit

Banks play a significant economic role in capitalist societies. They help direct excess money from those who temporarily do not need it to those who need it and provide sufficient guarantees. They have a significan role in the selection of projects according to their economic prospects Their role can be compared to that of the heart in the human body, which distributes oxygen-rich blood to the organs. As a critical element of a country's economy, each bank is subject to reasonably strict supervision by a supervisory authority to verify the financial institution's solidarity about the risks of credit and finances. The economy cannot deny the role of credit for trade facilitation, production stimulation, and development of amplification.

1. Credit Enables Exchanges

It is a former function of the banks to assure the companies a continuity in production and marketing. The purchasing or exchange power of companies originates from their recourse to the bank to anticipate their revenue.

2. Credit Stimulates Production

The dual role of credit lies in its power to stimulate production.

What does it mean? The production activity is modernizing day by day, thanks to innovation. The use of credit allows the company to acquire new technology, allowing it to increase the quality and quantity of its production. Households will consume the latter through consumer loans granted by banks to stimulate purchases and, consequently, the production sector.

3. Credit Boosts Development

Credit makes it possible to amplify development. Banking theory has evoked the multiplier role of credit, which is explained by the effects of a loan to purchase a production or consumption good. These effects are manifested not only by the economic agent benefiting from the operation but also indirectly to other agents. On the multiplier effect of credit in economic development, mention should be made of the contribution of JA Schumpeter concerning the study of the financing conditions of economic growth. Therefore, he will break with the classic analysis of the financing of investments (A. Smith), according to which only savings can carry out this financing. For JA Schumpeter, banks will finance investments by creating new means of payment and not by prior savings deposited with them. At the end of 2016, there were some 8.4 million consumer credit contracts in Belgium, i.e., warranties intended for private use (excluding mortgage loans).

This shows the importance of consumer credit in everyday life.

An essential cog in any economy, it also plays a significant positive social role.

The consumer can benefit from it.

The Consumer's Point of View

As a consumer, you use credit as a tool. Depending on the form it will take, it will allow you either to manage your budget more flexibly (we can think, for example, of the one-off money needs related to events such as a communion, a wedding) or to dissociate a purchase. Without credit, in the first case, you could be faced with monthly cash flow problems, while in the second, you would be forced to save the entire amount needed for your projects before carrying them out . . . at risk. You sometimes must give it up! Warning! In no case can credit be considered as an additional resource for the borrower. Credit is the lending of money with interest. Committing to a loan should be a thoughtful act, and it is better to avoid it if you are not sure you can repay, especially if you already have late payments or a structurally too-tight budget.

The Economic and Social Level

In a market economy, credit plays a central role. It is usually said that credit is the engine of the economy. Why? Because by facilitating access to consumer goods, it enables mass production, which leads to lower selling prices, which ultimately benefits the consumer.

Credit thus accelerates the life cycle of products and their accessibility to the most significant number through lower prices. Therefore, even those who buy in cash unknowingly benefit from the beneficial effects of credit!

In addition, credit is an essential provider of jobs. The financial sector is indirectly for all the sectors it supports (automotive, household equipment, construction, etc.). Credit, in addition to its economic function, also plays a social role.

How To Build Credit If You Don't Have It

Whether you're considering buying a car or applying for a mortgage, you'll need to have strong credit to get approved and get a low-interest rate. Even if you're looking for a job or department, having a low credit profile, which means you don't have enough credit history of generating a credit score, can prevent you from outperforming other applicants in the process. When you need to borrow money from a bank, your credit score is also used. Insurance companies, telephone service providers, and other businesses may charge you higher rates or additional fees if you have a low credit score. Building a good credit score can be challenging, especially if you're starting or your credit history is minimal. Unfortunately, many of our clients face this problem when they move abroad to seek new opportunities in another country and need to settle down. However, there are ways that you can build a good credit history from scratch. While it may be time-consuming, your efforts will show banks, landlords, and potential employers that you are a good prospect. It is essential to know everything that can be part of your credit score.

Why Good Credit is Important

Many companies use your credit history to predict your future financial behaviors because it shows how you've handled debt in the past. When you apply to borrow money, get a credit card, or rent an apartment, your credit history may be scrutinized. Good credit scores may indicate that you are responsible and have good financial habits, such as paying your bills on time. Credit scores, on the other hand, may also have the opposite effect. There is no one-size-fits-all method for determining creditworthiness. However, the Consumer Financial Protection Bureau suggests some ways to improve your credit. And Capital One has six tips for using credit cards responsibly that you might find helpful as well.

Five Situations in Which Credit Is Critical

Knowing when your credit will be reviewed can give you an idea of how critical it can be. Here are five scenarios in which your credit may be used:

1. Credit Card

When you apply for a credit card, the card issuer may run a credit check. Every business has its credit policies. However, having good credit may give you more options. If you are approved, having good credit may entitle you to benefits such as a higher credit limit and a lower annual percentage rate (APR). If you're trying to update a new card or request a higher credit limit on an existing card, your credit may also play a role.

2. Auto Loans and Mortgages

Credit is also essential when trying to buy a home or finance a car. Having good credit may help you qualify for a loan, and a loan with a lower interest rate. And interest rates are critical because the faster you pay, the more you may pay over the life of the loan. Consider recent thirty-year fixed-rate mortgage averages for a $200,000 loan. According to data from FICO®, a famous credit scoring company, payments can vary greatly. For example, FICO offers the following two estimates: A person with a credit score of 650, which FICO considers fair, would have a 3.566 percent APR and a monthly payment of $908. That $48 difference may not appear to be significant. However, it could add up to more than $17,000 throughout the loan. And this is based on a twenty-point difference in credit scores. As credit scores continue to rise, monthly payments may fall even further, increasing the difference in total costs.

3. Utilities and Insurance

Your credit history may even have an impact on how much you pay for insurance. However, insurers may use credit-based insurance scores instead of a traditional credit score in conjunction with other factors. Auto insurers, for example, may consider your age and the vehicle you drive. When you open accounts with utilities and cellphone providers, credit may be considered. You may be able to avoid paying deposits or be offered more favorable contract terms if you have good credit.

4. Housing Applications

When you apply for a lease to rent an apartment or a house, the landlord may inquire about your credit history as well as your criminal and rental records. Landlords frequently ask for permission to conduct screenings, but they are not always required to do so. Landlords may use these screenings to predict the type of tenant you will be. Even if your credit isnt perfect, you might be able to rent. However, if a landlord receives multiple applications, they may decide to rent to the fellow applicant being the fellow applicant may have better credit.

5. Job Applications

Some employers may request a background check if you apply for a job, including a credit check. It's widespread in jobs involving money or sensitive information. Background screening information can be used in a variety of ways, depending on the rules. In addition, companies must obtain your written permission before running a check. Moreover, if you refuse, you may not be considered for the position at all. There are no quick fixes for bad credit. Keeping track of your credit reports, on the other hand, is one way to ensure that potential employers are at least judging the correc information.

Why It Is Important to Establish Credit for Your Company

Good credit history will not only allow your company to raise funds to buy goods, acquire inventory, or expand its operations, but it will also allow it to access new business opportunities. In this sense, when you want to negotiate a contract orally with potential partners, your credit history will be considered. On the other hand, lenders want to know if you'll be able to pay them on time. As a result, they check your credit history and credit score on the major credit bureaus' websites. These indicators help banks determine whether you are trustworthy enough to lend money and at what interest rates.

How to start Generating Credit

Some people prefer to avoid credit because it seems too complicated and does not deserve their attention so early in life. The truth is that it is not wise to postpone it.

If you haven't had a credit card or loan, your record is blank. Therefore, it is not recorded anywhere that you can handle credit responsibly.

This can affect you when applying for credit in the future.

1. Open a Bank Account

If you want to get loans or a credit card, you should start by opening a bank account.

Although doing so is not mandatory, it will help your credit history.

2. Apply for a Secured Card or a Secured Loan

Apply for a secured loan or a secured credit card. Once you've applied for one of these two options, you must always make your payments on time. If you decide to apply for a loan, make sure you have a qualified co-debtor, a relative, or a legal representative on your side. The person will also oversee the loan you request.

3. Use the Card Very Carefully

To establish good credit history, try to use the card sparingly. Pay with it only the amount that you can contribute monthly. It is recommended that you do not use all the available credit; this way, you show that you manage your debts responsibly, and you will improve your credit score.

4. Order Credit Reports

There are agencies where you can order your credit reports: Equifax, Experian, and TransUnion, among them. Having used your credit for six months, check how your history is going. Check the positives and negatives so you can correct what you are failing in.

5. Other Credit Products

Look for other credit products. Other products can help you build a credit history. Lenders allow you to apply for a car loan or lease with the support of a qualified co-signer. Another option is an institution, which will allow you to place the money from the approved loan in a certificate of deposit to which you will pay for the term you choose. When paying off your loan, the bank will disburse the money from your certificate, in addition to the interest generated. This process of building credit is something that takes time. You must be responsible with your financial decisions and have a lot of patience because the best way to make your credit is little by little. This will help you build a solid track record without overcommitting borrowing large amounts or too many cards. Remember, it is not just about paying your debts on time; it is essential to build a solid financial future, Including saving for your retirement.

Do you want more advice for your financial future? Here are some links to refer to for more tips https://privilegecreditconsultants.com https://www.nerdwallet.com https://wallethub.com

11 Ways to Build Credit for Your Business

Here are ten practices that will help you establish or improve the credit profile of your company.

1. Apply for a Business Credit Card

An excellent way to generate business credit is to obtain a credit card from a bank that reports your payments to the main credit bureaus. It is convenient to have at least one, but you can have several if it suits you financially. If you don't have a credit history, it's a good idea to apply for a secured credit card, which, unlike an unsecured one, can be approved without credit. Be careful though, don't exceed your credit limits—it doesn't matter if you have funds; that doesn't mean you should use all of them. You must stop using your card for business expenses once you have a business credit card. While using your credit card may be more convenient, it will not improve your business credit.

Start building your business credit now if you intend to apply for a business loan in the future. Avoid the use of personal credit cards, personal auto loans, and personal credit in general if you need cash for your business. But don't worry if you don't want to get a business credit card; it's not your only option. Continue reading!

2. Separate your Personal Expenses from Your Business Expenses

First, make sure your business is properly Incorporated. You won't be able to build business credit on your credit score alone. Also, you must never use a business bank account for your personal expenses. You need to see your business as a separate entity and learn to identify your expenses. Separating your business expenses and your personal expenses is not only advisable, but it is also necessary. Charging your expenses to your business account can indeed be a way to reduce your taxes. Also, it is easier to manage a single bank account than to have them separate. But it is a practice that can harm you in the long term, and that can make it difficult to obtain commercial credit. You may be wondering how this can be possible. How does combining your business and personal expenses affect your eligibility for a loan?

This is what happens: when your lender studies your business account statement, it will show very little cash flow (the amount that results from subtracting your expenses and cash withdrawals from your deposits, which will result in reduced loan/credit eligibility or not being eligible at all. In other words, there is no room to add one more debt, like that of a loan. Vector illustration of influential investor giving money supporting businessman in future development. Concept: credit for small business

3. Acquire a Federal Employer Identification Number

The Federal Employer Identification Number (also known as EIN for its English abbreviation) is your company's social security number. You'll need one to open a bank account in your company's name or to sign commercial contracts. To obtain this number, you must register on the IRS website and with your Secretary of State.

4. Acquire a D-U-N-S Number

You must visit the Dun & Bradstreet Credibility Corporation agency site to get a D-U-N-S- Number (Unique 9 Digit Identifier for business), with which your business will be added to a database of millions of companies, thus allowing your company's credit history to be consulted by your potential customers, banks, and potential business partners.

5. Put Your Business on The Map

You cannot build credit effectively until you have established your business. Make sure your business name, address, and email are up to date. Get a business phone number and have it listed in the directory.

6. Establish Credit Lines with Your Suppliers

A solid line of credit with your key suppliers is worth its weight in gold in the business world. Many vendors provide this type of benefit, allowing you to pay for your supplies several days or weeks after receiving them.

By establishing a line of credit with vendors who report your payments to the business credit bureaus, you can build a positive credit history.

Moreover, these providers are not required to report your payments to the agencies; therefore, you should ask them to write them or be proactive and open accounts only with those who submit the information.

7. Update Your Information with The Credit Bureaus

As we mentioned in a previous article, several credit bureaus oversee collecting information and creating business credit scores, such as Experian and Equifax. They all have a different method for calculating scores, and each bank and financial institution reports additional data to these agencies.

As you do not know which agency your suppliers, creditors, or potential clients will review, the best thing to do is update your information in all of them. Dun & Bradstreet, for example, allows owners to update basic information about their businesses, such as years in operation or number of employees, and publish their financial statements on the platform. The more complete your profile, the better.

8. Check Your Credit Report Frequently

Twenty-five percent of small business owners report significant errors on their credit reports. Reading your credit history carefully can help you detect any problems or inaccuracies. If you find an error, you must file a complaint with the appropriate agency.

In any case, remember that if you stop paying your taxes, have been sued, or have declared bankruptcy, all this information will go directly to your report, negatively affecting your credit score.

9. Always Pay on Time

Or better yet, pay before!

When you pay bills on time, you show that your business is trustworthy and can effectively manage your debts. If you default, your creditors can send adverse reports to the credit bureaus. History of defaults or delays can affect your chances of accessing loans and damaging your credibility with other companies and consumers.

10. Deposit Cash Transactions in Your Business Bank Account

Even if you do all your transactions in cash, deposit it in your business bank account. You have no other way to show the size of your business or that it is growing. Also, keeping your money under the mattress is simply not safe, nor is it the wisest option. Going to your closest branch to deposit all your cash should be part of your routine. Do it once a week or as often as you need. Once you start putting this into practice, you will monitor and manage your cash flow much better. And there is nothing more important than having a clear vision of the direction your business is taking. What happens if you don't deposit your company's cash in your company's bank account? Then all this capital will not be considered when requesting a loan, which can lead to being denied or being granted a much lower amount than you deserve. A growing business has a better chance of being approved as well as a higher loan amount. It makes sense, right?

11. Give Yourself a Salary

Yes, you are the owner, and it is about your business, so you should have the authority and freedom to withdraw money from your business wherever you want, right? No! You must follow the rules. Your company's bank account should be used only for your business purposes, such as paying your employees and suppliers or buying inventory. But if you don't have a lot of personal income, consider assigning yourself a salary. Assign your-self a monthly payment of the W-2 or 1099 category. Yes, you can be one more employee in your own company. Your company is a separate entity, and you must see it that way. Also, giving yourself a W-2 or 1099 income can improve your credit and your chances of being approved for a busi-ness loan. Your lender may consider this salary an additional source of income. And the added income means not only a better chance of being approved and a higher loan amount. You will win in any way. Don't worry about starting a salary in the beginning you need to study the situation, perhaps using an accountant or someone who can assess your company's case to determine how much your salary should be. Or you can analyze the problem yourself and conclude.

Methods for Increasing Your Credit Score

It takes time to build credit. There are aspects you can do to instantly improve your credit score from poor to excellent. You need to gradually add new credit and make your monthly payments on time.

With this method, you should start building your path to a good credit score in six months to a year. Still, there are other ways to build credit besides giving you time and making your payments. Here are some ways to start building the recognition of your dreams:

1. Report Your Income and Other Data

Do you pay your rent on time? You can ask the landlord to report this to the credit bureaus. On-time payments are suitable for your credit, but they frequently go unreported. Utility bill payments and other positive financial data can also be reported. Experian Boost is a free service that allows you to quickly improve your credit score by linking payment histories from other accounts.

2. Become an Authorized User

How to build credit; most credit card companies (will report an authorized user's credit history to credit bureaus. If a family member or friend is willing to add you as an authorized user, make sure to check with the credit card company first to ensure that the history will be reported to the credit bureaus. Next you want to ensure that the account doesn't have any late payments or high balances (Revolving balance should not be more than 20% of credit limit). If that's the case, you can become an authorized user and build credit that way.

3. Use a Co-Debtor

Lenders will let you sign a loan with someone who has better credit than you. This means that if you are unable to pay, they will be obligated to repay the loan. Having a co-debtor can also lower your interest rate and improve your chances of being approved if your credit is not as good or established. Before asking someone to cosign, make sure you can afford it You don't want to sully someone else's credit while attempting to establish your own!

4. Apply for a Secured Loan or a Credit-Building Loan

A credit-building loan is explicitly designed to assist you in improving your credit. When you obtain a loan, the bank places it on a Certificate of Deposit (CD) that they control. A CD is a savings account that earns interest over time, allowing you to save while building credit. Then, just like any other loan, you make monthly payments.

5. Apply for a Secured Credit Card

A secured credit card means paying a deposit before you spend. The amount of your deposit becomes your credit limit on the card. Secured credit cards don't require good credit to qualify. These are generally the most accessible cards to get if you don't have credit.

Why You Should Establish Credit

If you've always paid for purchases with cash or checks and have never used credit, getting started is a good idea. It's critical to repair your credit history for several reasons: You may need a good credit history for routine matters, such as connecting the utilities at your home. Good credit history is essential in obtaining financing when buying furniture, a computer, a car, or a new home. Employers could verify prospective employees' credit ratings. Renting an apartment may be easier if you have a good credit score because landlords know you are more likely to pay your rent on time each month. If you need a loan, banks may look more favorably on you if you have a good credit score credit history.

Personal Credit vs. Business Credit

Credit score ranges exist for both business and personal credit. Business credit scores typically range from 1 to 100, with 100 representing the highest available score. Individual credit scores usually range from 350 to 850, with 850 representing the highest available score. The higher your credit score, the more likely you are to qualify for better terms, such as lower interest rates and larger loans.

How Business Credit is Calculated

Business credit considers various factors, including the length of time your company has been in operation, vendor accounts, lines of credit, open credit card accounts, annual income, loans, liens, and public information. However, each factor may have a different weight depending on the credit bureaus and the scoring model.

How Personal Credit is Calculated

The Five Cs of credit are five significant factors that influence your credit score.

- **Payment History (35%)**
- **Credit Utilization (30%)**
- **Length of Credit History (15%)**
- **Credit Mix (10%)**
- **New Credit Accounts (10%)**

Your payment history and credit utilization rate account for sixty-five percent of your credit score.

How to Build Personal Credit

You can start building and improving your credit by paying off existing debts, opening a personal credit card, and making payments on time. Your payment history and credit utilization rate are the two most important factors that make up your credit score. Generally, your total balances should never exceed thirty percent of your entire available credit.

Credit Card Description

A credit card is a thin rectangular piece of plastic or metal issued by a bank or financial services company that allows cardholders to borrow money and use it to buy goods and services from merchants who accept credit cards. Credit cards require cardholders to repay the borrowed funds fully, plus any applicable interest and any additional agreed-upon charges, by the billing date or over time. The Chase Sapphire Reserve is an example of a credit card. More to the standard credit line, the credit card company may offer cardholders a separate cash line of credit (LOC), which allows them to borrow money in the form of cash advances that can be accessed through bank tellers, ATMs, or credit card convenience checks. Compared to transactions that access the main credit line, such cash advances typically have different terms, such as no grace period and higher interest rates. Issuers usually pre-set borrowing limits based on an individual's credit rating. Many businesses let customers make purchases with credit cards, which remain one of today's most popular payment methodologies for buying consumer goods and services.

A credit card is distinguished from a charge card in that the balance must be paid in full each month or at the end of each statement cycle. On the other hand, credit cards allow consumers to accumulate a continuing debt balance subject to interest.

A credit card is also distinguished from a charge card in that it typically involves a third-party entity that pays the seller and is reimbursed by the buyer. On the other hand, a charge card simply defers the buyer's payment until a later date.

How a credit card can help you

A credit card can be a great place to start when it comes to building credit. You can make purchases with your credit card; they are very convenient. One way to start building a credit history is to have a department store or gas station card or two.

They allow you to:

- **Shop online or over the phone when cash may not be an option**
- **Make travel reservations, buy airline tickets, and rent cars. Rental car companies might require a hold or deposit if you don't use a credit card.**
- **Shop safer without carrying a lot of cash**
- **Budget for more significant purchases by paying in installments**
- **Access funds for emergency needs**

Credit Cards vs. Debit Cards

Credit and debit cards are almost identical in appearance, with sixteen-digit card numbers, expiration dates, magnetic strips, and EMV chips. With one key difference, both can make it simple and convenient to make purchases in stores or online. Debit cards enable you to spend money by drawing funds from your bank account. Credit cards will allow you to borrow money from the card issuer to a specific limit to purchase goods or withdraw cash.

In your wallet, you most likely have at least one credit card and one debit card. The convenience and protection they provide are difficult to beat, but significant differences could have a substantial impact on your wallet. Here's how to figure out which one to use based on your spending requirements.

Benefits of Using a Credit Card

Some of the benefits include:

- **Convenience**- Using a credit card lets you buy something today but puts off the actual cost until payday rolls around so you don't have to wait.
- **Spread out the costs**- If you want to make a huge purchase, a credit card allows you to pay in monthly installments. This can help with budgeting and won't put a massive dent in your finances.
- **Improving your credit score**- Lenders will notice if you use your credit card responsibly, which can help improve your credit score. If you have a small credit score, you can apply for a credit builder credit card designed to help you improve your credit score.
- **Purchase protection**- Sometimes there could be a problem with your purchase—it might get lost or damaged, for example, or the company could even go bust. With credit cards, you have buyer protection for purchases made on the card. It means you can claim your money back from the card provider if there's an issue with your goods or services.
- **Interest-free**- Plenty of credit cards offer a zero-percent interest period. That means you can borrow for free, with no interest charged, so long as you make your minimum monthly repayments.
- **Cashback and rewards**- Many credit card providers offer a range of incentives to customers. You could be getting air miles or similar shopper loyalty points each time you use your card or even cashback on purchases.
- **Slim down your debts**- If you're already paying off debts, you could use a balance transfer credit card to reduce your interest payments, helping you clear your debt quicker.

Disadvantages of Credit Cards

Getting a credit card can come with pitfalls and drawbacks. Some of the risks you should be aware of include:

- **You are getting trapped in debt**. If you can't pay back what you borrow, your debts can pile up quickly. If you have bad credit, you could get hit with high interest rates, and once you're in spiraling debt, it can be challenging to pay it all off.

You are damaging your credit. Your credit score can go down as well as up. Miss a payment on your card or allow debt to stack up, and this can damage your credit rating. This can make it harder to get credit in the future.

- **Extra fees.** The interest rate isn't the only number you need to look out for when choosing a credit card—there may be additional charges. Your provider could impose fees if you miss a payment or go over your credit limit, which is bad news if you're already in the red. Some credit cards might have a monthly or annual fee, and many balance transfer cards charge a fee to switch a balance. Check the APR (annual percentage rate) to get an idea of the overall cost of a card.
- **Limited use**. Credit card providers might charge you extra for things that are free with a debit card, such as withdrawing cash from an ATM or buying things overseas.

Best Way to Use your Credit Card

Different types of credit cards will suit different people, depending on whether they want to pay off existing debt quickly, make a large one-off purchase, or earn cashback on weekly spending. Here are some helpful tips to make sure you're getting the best from your card:

- **Pick the right card**

There are many different types of cards to choose from, so consider your needs before deciding. If you want to spread out a significant expense, a purchase card could be right for you. Are you looking to pay less on your existing debts? Try a balance transfer card. Our guide to finding the right card could help with your decision.

- **Balance the books**

In general, you should never charge anything to your credit card that you can't afford to pay back later. Spending within your means keeps your credit score healthy, and it'll stop you from falling into debt.

- **Pay over the minimum**

It's crucial to meet your minimum monthly repayment, but ideally, try to pay back more. If you can afford to pay off more than the minimum, it's a good move because you'll pay less in interest. Plus, if you can clear the balance each month, you shouldn't pay any claim, and you won't have to worry about falling into debt.

- **Get a direct debit**

You won't have to remember to make your monthly payments if you set up a direct debit. Set it to the minimum monthly amount, but remember, paying off more is usually better.

- **Stay alert**

Most providers will offer an alert system, by text or online, so you'll know when a payment is due or if you're approaching your credit limit.

- **Pick up some perks**

If you're using a rewards card, make sure you take full advantage of all the extras. These cards tend to come with an annual fee, so you could be losing money if you don't use them enough. For example, you could use your cashback credit card for all your regular daily purchases, then pay off the balance in full each month, but reap the rewards.

- **Your applications should be carefully considered**

If you need to get a credit or debit card, you can leave a mark on your credit report, and making too many applications in a short period is generally regarded as a sign of poor financial health. Timing your applications and using Money Super Market's credit card eligibility checker— so you can search for card deals without harming your credit rating—can boost your chance of being accepted.

Factors to Consider When Choosing a Credit Card

When choosing a credit card, it's essential to consider what you'd like to do with your new card.

Maybe you have some significant expenses coming up, and you want to break up the cost into more manageable chunks. You might want to pay down your existing debts, or maybe you'd like to earn cashback or rewards.

With Nerd Wallet, it's easy to find the best credit card for you. Once you've started your search, here are a few things to look out for:

1. Fee-Free Overseas

Think about whether you're likely to need to use the card abroad. Some cards allow you to send money abroad without extra charges.

2. Credit Limits

Consider what is a sensible credit limit for you. A high credit limit can provide added flexibility, but a lower limit could reduce the risk of getting into debt.

3. Extra Charges

There could be added fees on certain cards, particularly those offering perks and cashback. Weigh up if the price is worth paying for the benefit. Many cards are showing zero percent interest for different periods, sometimes up to two years or longer. If this is important to you, remember to compare other deals and consider any add-on fees.

Compare Credit Cards with Nerd Wallet

Finding the right credit card is easy with this tool.

When you create an account, and enter some personal information, you'll see which cards you're most likely to be accepted for. Once you've found the card you want, just click through to the provider to finalize your application. The lender will tell you your credit limit and the interest rate. As soon as your new card comes through the mail, you'll just need to activate it, then it will be ready to use.

What is Financial Planning?

In the field of administration and finance, the process of determining how an organization, company, or person will manage its capital resources to achieve its established objectives is known as financial planning. In simpler terms, it is developing a financial plan, i.e., a budget and a scheme of expenses that allows organizing, managing money effectively and conveniently. This financial planning process must consider deadlines, costs, and objectives in a detailed, personalized, and organized way, for which it usually uses the following stages:

Establishment of objectives and their priority expressed in financial terms. Definition of the deadlines to achieve these objectives. Prepare a financial budget that identifies the items (or money segments) necessary to meet the objectives.

Measurement and control of financial decisions taken and their comparison with previous financial plans. In this way, financial planning is usually exercised in advance, to organize the economic future of the organization, usually at the hands of financial advisers and expense planners, either their own or outsourced.

Types of financial planning

- **Short-term**- financial planning encompasses projections of one year or less. Based on its temporal scope, we can quickly distinguish two types of financial planning, which are:
- **Long-term**- financial planning. These are generally projections between two and five years in the future, so they are handled with a much greater range of variables and uncertainty, requiring more general approaches.

Importance of financial planning

Financial planning is a vital tool for companies and organizations, especially when making decisions. Like people, companies have a budget and certain financial limitation within whose margins they must manage to achieve their objectives.

Hence, a careful plan of how to invest money is always a good idea.

Difference Between Assets and Liabilities

The difference between assets and liabilities is based on the nature they possess at an economic level. While an asset will generate a property or a collection right in our finances, a liability will produce a payment obligation.

In other words, the main difference between an asset and a liability is that the former will be able to generate income, and the latter will only originate an expense.

Definition of Asset

Assets are all the assets, investments, and rights that the company has and is classified as:

Current assets

Are goods and investments of a transitory nature or convertible into money within a certain time frame. The existing assets are classified in order of availability and are composed of:

- **Cash and Cash Equivalents**
- **Inventory**
- **Investments**
- **Vehicles**
- **Brands and Patents**
- **Accounts Receivable**
- **Land**
- **Furniture and Equipment**
- **Long-Term Investments**

Noncurrent Assets or Fixed Assets

Assets that, for different reasons, are very difficult to convert into cash because they are not liquid and that the company usually keeps for periods of more than one year.

Depreciation

Represents the loss of value suffered by assets due to use or over time and is recorded as a supplementary asset account (negative), reducing the support that gives rise to it.

Deferred Assets

The balance of the deferred asset accounts is made up of expenses paid n advance, on which you have the right to receive a good service, both n the same year and in subsequent years. The deferred asset is made up of:

- **Amortizable Investments (organization expenses and installation expenses)**
- **Prepaid Advertising**
- **Bond Issuance Costs**
- **Prepaid Insurance**
- **Prepaid Rent**

Definition of Liabilities

Represents the debts and obligations of a company or person. Some examples are:

- **Auto Loans**
- **Mortgages**
- **Secured Personal Loans**
- **Unsecured Personal Loans**
- **Student Loans**

Stockholders' Equity:

Stockholders' equity is shareholders' equity, i.e., the residual interest in the assets after deducting all liabilities include contributions made, either the time of incorporation or at later times, as well as retained earnings and is formed by the following accounts:

- **Social Capital (contributions)**
- **Legal Reserve**
- **Retained or Accumulated Earnings**
- **Net Income (Loss) for the year**

Relationship Between Assets, Liabilities, and Equity?

Assets are equal to the sum of the company's liabilities and shareholders' equity

Formula (Assets = Liabilities + Equity)

The theory indicates that a company's assets are financed with third-party funds (liabilities) or its funds (equity).

- **Assets**- Assets and Collection Rights
- **Liabilities**- Obligations and Debts
- **Equity**- Capital and Profits

We can affirm that liability can allow us to obtain an asset that would take much longer to receive if it were exclusively through pure savings and without any indebtedness.

More Examples of Assets and Liabilities

To see in a more practical way what an asset and a liability consist of in our daily lives, here are some more detailed examples of each along with their function:

Laptop- It is a good that we own. We can take advantage of it by using it for work or leisure. You can make money by selling it. Therefore, it is an asset.

- **Housing**- It is good that we own. We can earn an income by selling or renting it which would make it an asset.

- **Mortgage Loan-** It is a payment obligation. It allows us to get a home without having saved the total purchase value which makes it a liability.
- **Personal loan-** In this case, it is also a payment obligation. It allows us to obtain a sum of funding and pay it back over time.
- **Debt Issuance-** It asks the market for borrowed money in exchange for periodic payment obligations by the company that issues it which makes it a liability. Although there are more examples that we could explain, these are the most common and will come up the most in daily life.

What Is a D-U-N-S Number?

The DUNS number (Data Universal Numbering System) is a nine-digit identifier that provides a unique identity to each company internationally. It is a system that is developed and regulated by the American company Dun & Bradstreet (D&B). Currently, this system identifies more than 300 million companies worldwide and their business relationships (both hierarchies and links).

What is the D-U-N-S Number for?

There are almost no frontiers to international trade in a global economy like the one we find ourselves in. However, each country has its tax standards to identify its companies and guarantee the stability of international transactions, which often makes operations difficult.

The DUNS numbers try to solve this problem. It is the equivalent of the national identifier but on a global scale (in Spain, it is the CIF), which allows the standardization of identification numbers to track companies on a worldwide scale. This identifier is assigned to all types of entities, whether private companies, government entities, nonprofit organizations, corporations, and all kinds of associations. It consists of nine digits, and you can use hyphens or not to separate them (in the format XXX-XXX-XXX). Once a D-U-N-S number is assigned to a business, it is permanent, even if it goes bankrupt.

D-U-N-S numbers began to be used in 1963, although only to identify the internal financial reports of the D&B company. Later, its use became general and extended to all companies internationally and, today, it is the standard that governs the identification of companies between different countries.

Why should companies have a D-U-N-S number?

Having a D-U-N-S number is not required, but it is recommended. They are spreading more and more in international operations, especially in business with North American companies. For example, some American government agencies require that the supplier company be assigned a D-U-N-S number.

You will also need it if you want to open a business account with some services of large U.S. companies, for example, as part of the registration process for the Apple Developer Program.

In Europe, although it is not yet so widespread, it is becoming more and more critical, mainly due to the increase in commercial operations between our continent and North America.

Budget

A budget refers to the amount of money needed to meet a certain number of expenses necessary to undertake a project in economics. In this way, it can be defined as an anticipated figure that estimates the cost that the achievement of said objective will entail.

In other words, the budget is the delimitation in monetary terms of the conditions surrounding the chosen project and the results that are expected to be achieved after its completion within a specified time. Therefore, this quantitative expression, in turn, supposes a high level of unity with the business plan and the strategies that mark the path of the company.

Period Of a Budget

About the period we are talking about, it is possible to classify the different types of budgets between short-term planning (typical of daily projects and faster) and long-term (more common in the activity of large companies or the countries' economic policies) planning.

The annual budgets of a company are usually expressed with the following periods:

- **First trimester**- In English, it is associated with "quarter". it is usually referred to as Q1.
- **Second trimester**- It is usually referred to as Q2.
- **Third trimester**- It is usually referred to as Q3.
- **Fourth trimester**- It is usually referred to as Q4.

Each trimester has three months, and therefore, they complete a whole year of twelve months.

In other words, the budget can be understood to mark the action plan that the company will carry out, defining the objectives that are sought n the said task and the functions that are necessary to carry out to achieve them. In this sense, it is common for budgets to present a series of common characteristics, such as predictability, cheapness, flexibility, reliability, participation, and opportunity.

Budget Types

Budgeting is essential for the correct use of the resources available to the company, which can be efficiently assigned and used if this type of prior planning is available. In this way, it is easier to measure the risk related to these types of objectives to reduce it as much as possible and achieve better results.

On the other hand, a budget can also act as an informal method for public institutions and bodies. The eight types of budgets that exist are:

- **Master Budget**
- **Operating Budget**
- **Sales Budget**
- **Production Budget**
- **Shopping Budget**
- **Cash Flow Budget**
- **Treasury Budget**
- **Marketing Budget**

1. Master budget

The master budget collects all budgets to create a comprehensive financial picture. Therefore, it covers all the information. It includes the economic data for the budgeted cash flow, and everything related to the financial and economic base to achieve the main objective.

- **What is that goal?** It is to maintain balance in the relationship of the various departments of the company. From this perspective, it will encourage the functionality of the processes and contribute to achieving the goals of the entire business. This budget comprises two critical areas: the operating budget and the financial budget, which we will explain below.

2. Operating Budget

This budget includes the production, sales, and administrative activities of the company. It focuses on collecting and analyzing essential data such as income, expenses, the actual statement of profit or loss focused on the future. Large-scale companies commonly use it. It starts from the complexity of the operations and occurs in each period.

In this budget, sales, sales price, production budget, raw material requisitions, labor, manufacturing expenses, administration expenses, among others, coexist. The much more efficient way to carry out these finances is to summarize them in a report with organized data from each department. This allows the organization to have up-to-date data on where operating budgets are going through an income statement.

3. Sales Budget

It is also known as the revenue budget and defines what the organization is expected to do in the market. It is adjusted to the demand, and based on that principle, a production budget is prepared that contains an approach to future goals and the increase in the company's equity.

Most companies carry out this procedure, keeping all economic data up to date, which is crucial for sound financial management. In many cases, it is even the first step to create budgets.

To make a sales budget, we recommend clarifying the goals you want to achieve with sales in a specific period. Make an objective study using an instrument that allows you to evaluate the demand that exists in the market. This way, you can guarantee a correct analysis of factors such as the economy, the industry, the data collected from the sales in the past, and the sector to facilitate the execution once the budget has been accepted. After this, you must communicate it to all the departments involved.

4. Production Budget

It is the backbone of your business budget. It is done after the sales budget because they are closely related. With the data collection of both, it is foreseen how much should be produced and if the results agree with the expected objectives. This is of utmost importance since the leaders in charge of its management will know what is being manufactured. They will see the plan of input and resource requirements for the effective growth of the profit in the organization and the calculation of the cost destined for sales. Those in charge of this budget are usually senior management, as they must adequately execute the factors involved in the process. Labor and raw materials are two main aspects to consider in this budget.

5. Purchase Budget

It is also known as a raw material needs budget. It is done after the production budget. The costs of the inputs that a company requires for production and sale can be found in an orderly manner.

To do this efficiently, implement an inventory that helps you determine the needs of the different inputs. It considers essential aspects such as the exact standard of each product, the number of times they will be required, the efficient supply of enough materials to avoid shortages, and the unit price.

The purchasing budget must have this data updated so that the order scheduling (considering the delivery time) is flourishing and obtaining the necessary raw material to produce.

6. Cash Flow Budget

This is closely related to the treasury budget (which you will see later). Its main objective is to establish the flow of money that a company has in each period. It is of utmost importance for strategic decision making because it reflects how much and how the money comes in. This allows you to plan correctly. With this budget, you will be considering all the information to define whether the business has the monetary resources to continue operating and how these resources are managed. The cash budget provides essential data to know the final figures and know if you have a surplus or deficit of cash. The data that will facilitate the collection of information are the following:

- **Ticket Flow**
- **Output Flow**
- **Net Cash Flow**
- **Final Cash**
- **Excess Cash Balance**

7. Treasury Budget

This budget is one of the most important if you want to generate more significant economic growth in your company. Control and anticipate the financial values that the organization owns. It contemplates a future vision that consists of collecting data on collections, payments, and expenses to define if they can be met with the income obtained by the business. Also, plan the steps to follow in case of mismatches, such as excess or deficit of liquidity.

The ideal times to make this budget are at the beginning of the business activity and the financial year. Knowing exactly how you can obtain this budget is by considering the capital inflow minus the expenses. For this reason, this budget is divided into two types:

8. Collection's Budget

It is based on collecting data through the entries and possible entries expected to be available to the company. It is usually confused with the income budget. Still, in this case, the charges represent the inflow of liquid money that you obtain from sales, transfers, or capital contributions and various ways. The deadlines to be finalized can last months or years, depending on the complexity of the agreement. Something important to consider when you make this budget, you should stick to reality as much as possible since you need to integrate all the criteria to have at your disposal, the money necessary for the company in the previously stipulated period.

9. Expense Budget

It refers to the exit or possible exit of money that your company has for movements necessary for production. In this budget, you must consider payments to suppliers, planned purchases, salaries, licenses, and various services constantly consumed. In this way, you can design more effective strategies for timely financial management. That is why it must be continuously reviewed and updated. To effectively carry out this budget, consider frequent ordinary payments such as social security contributions, cost of supplies, tax payments, and advertising and marketing.

Do not forget the business policies to adhere to the standard time managed by the organization. With this, you can cope with the constant operation and any additional expenses that may arise on the go.

10. Marketing Budget

It is focused on the various media with which your company interacts to advertise and create marketing strategies. This budget is essential to reach your customers and create an effective communication design. You must be concrete in your objectives and have data with exact numerical figures to have achievable goals.

You must always establish the amount of money that you will allocate to events, online advertising, websites, traditional media, agencies, among others. The main objective is to obtain the necessary data of the expenses you will spend acquiring said services during a specific time. This way, you will define if your budget is adjusted to the costs when starting your marketing strategy. To know your adequate marketing budget, you must attend to the promotion needs that the market demands of you. Compare with past budgets if it is not the first time you make this budget. The data you collect will allow you to compare it to previous years' sales. On that line, you can make intelligent decisions and establish a percentage equivalent to the sales forecast.

You can also check the competition to create a budget that allows you to increase your presence against other brands in the market. Do not forget to choose well the medium to which you will distribute your budget. This way, you will obtain the necessary information to incorporate the appropriate medium into your target market efficiently.

FICO Scores Vs. VantageScore

A credit score is a snapshot of your credit risk at a specific point in time. It can assist lenders in determining whether lending you money is a good investment.

Given that both the FICO and VantageScore serve the same purpose, its not surprising that they share several features.

1. Bureau Specific Models

FICO creates bureau-specific models. They offer one model for each major credit bureau.

VantageScore offers a single tri-bureau model that can be used for all 3 bureaus

2. Range of Credit Scores

FICO Scores range between 300 and 850. Initially, Vantage Scores had a different numerical scale (501 to 990). Vantage Score Models 3.0 and 4.0, on the other hand, used the same 300–850 scale as FICO.

Higher scores are better in both the FICO and Vantage Score models. Higher credit scores make it easier to qualify for financing and receive competitive loan offers from lenders. A good credit score can save you tens of thousands, if not hundreds of thousands, of dollars throughout your life.

3. Goal of Design

Credit score creators build their scoring models to perform a specific function.

This is referred to as the scoring model's stated design objective. FICO and Vantage Scores have the same indicated design goal. They can forecast whether a consumer will pay any credit obligation 90 days late or more within the next two years.

A higher credit score indicates that you are less likely to pay your bills severely late (90 days or more after the due date) shortly (the next 24 months). A lower credit score indicates the inverse.

4. Compliance with the ECOA

The scoring model must pass some tests before a lender can use it to evaluate applicants. It must comply with a federal law known as the Equal Credit

Opportunity Act (ECOA).

According to the ECOA, credit scores used for lending purposes in the United States must be empirically derived, demonstrably valid, and statistically sound. These terms imply that credit scores in the United States must be built using a tried and-true scientific method (aka empirically derived), and they must work (aka demonstrably and statistically sound).

A credit score should predict the likelihood of someone paying a bill ninety days or later in the next twenty-four months. As a result, FICO and VantageScore Solutions must demonstrate that each credit-scoring model they develop performs as intended.

5. Differences Between FICO Scores and VantageScore

Even though FICO Scores and VantageScore serve similar functions, they are not the same. Consider them the Pepsi and Coca-Cola of the financial world. The following are some critical distinctions between the two credit score brands.

FICO and VantageScore Solutions are two companies founded by FICO that compete with one another. Each of these companies creates and sells credit scores to lenders and other financial institutions.

FICO is a California-based publicly traded company. Bill Fair, an engi-neer, and

Earl Isaac, a mathematician, founded the analytics firm in 1956. Equifax, TransUnion, and Experian established VantageScore Solutions in Connecticut in

2006.

6. Criteria for minimum scoring

Everyone does not have access to a credit score. Your credit report must first meet the minimum criteria of a scoring model to receive one.

To be eligible for a FICO Score, your credit report must show a trace-line (e.g., credit card, loan, line of credit, etc.) at least six months old. In addition, at least one tradeline on your report must have shown activity within the last six months. It's a little easier to get a VantageScore now. Regardless of the age of the account, your credit report only requires at least one tradeline to be present.

Other forms of payment may be accepted if you do not have a credit card. Experian Boost, for example, may help you ensure that you have every opportunity to establish a credit profile.

7. Value of Points

A credit-scoring model examines your credit report and assigns you several points based on the information it discovers. You can earn points for each factor that the scoring model considers (e.g., payment history, credit utilization, length of credit history, credit inquiries, etc.). For example, a credit report with no late payments is worth X number of points added to your overall score. The items found on your credit report are assigned different values (or weights) by the FICO and VantageScore models. Your credit report may earn you 150 points toward your FICO Score if it is free of delinquencies. However, the same word with no late payments could earn you 155 points according to the VantageScore scoring model. These point values are purely speculative, but they do represent how credit scores work.

8. Credit Score Amounts

As previously stated, FICO and VantageScore credit scores have the same range of 300 to 850. Higher risk scores indicate lower risk. However, lenders' interpretations of the two types of scores may differ. Depending on the lender, the meaning of success credit score varies. It may also vary depending on the credit score brand. A 670 FICO Score, for example, maybe sufficient to qualify for a credit card from ABC Bank. However, for a different credit card issuer to approve your application, you may need a credit score of 680 VantageScore.

FICO and VantageScore Criteria

VantageScore and FICO credit-scoring models generate credit scores based on information obtained from consumer credit reports. However, depending on the model used, the data may have a different effect on the scores. Let's look at the critical factors that those models consider when calculating your scores.

VantageScore

- Age and credit type both have a lot of sways
- The percentage of credit limit used is highly influential
- Debt and total balances are moderately influential

- **Credit activity and inquiries in the last few months have been less influential**
- **Credit available is less influential**

FICO

Divides the data into five categories, each representing a percentage of your overall score.

- **Payment history (35%)**
- **Total amount owed (30%)**
- **Credit History (15%)**
- **New Credit (10%)**
- **Credit Mix (10%)**

However, keep in mind that the precise impact a specific category will have on your credit scores will vary depending on your personal credit history and the credit scoring model used.

What is a Pie Chart?

The pieces of the graph are proportional to the percentage of the total in each category. In other words, the size of each pie slice corresponds to the size of that category within the group overall. The "pie" represents the entire total, whereas the "slices" represent portions of the whole.